Instant Guitar Chords

864 Chords

24 Chord-types shown for every key,
each in 3 positions on the neck,
suitable for *Folk, Pop, Rock* and *Jazz*

by John Loesberg

OSSIAN

Published by

Ossian Publications

8/9 Frith Street, London W1D 3JB, UK

Exclusive Distributors:

Music Sales Limited

Distribution Centre, Newmarket Road,

Bury St. Edmunds, Suffolk IP33 3YB, UK

Music Sales Corporation

257 Park Avenue South, New York, NY10010

United States Of America

Music Sales Pty Limited

120 Rothschild Avenue,

Rosebery, NSW 2018, Australia

Order No. OMB60

ISBN 0-946005-46-X

This book © Copyright 1989, 2006 Novello & Company Limited,

part of The Music Sales Group.

www.musicsales.com

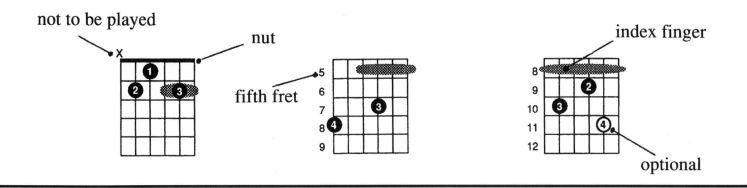

I always felt there was a need for something like this — a quick-reference book of chords that should enable the average player to find that odd chord in a hurry. When using this book keep in mind that there are no hard or fast rules for chord-shapes — the same chords may appear in various inversions and permutations. The technically correct names of the chords generally tend to reflect their pianistic origins which explains why many cannot in practice be fingered on the guitar. To make up for this however, the guitar's tone-colours and playing possibilities are infinitely more subtle than those of the keyboard.

Keep in mind too that the chords here are only a handful compared to the thousands that are there and many others that may be created.

Feel free to experiment with bass notes and see which strings to leave out. Strings marked with an X are generally to be avoided, others may or may not be useful — it all depends on the music and the mood — try picking different parts of the chord.

Yours chordially,*

John Loesberg

*Sorry about that.

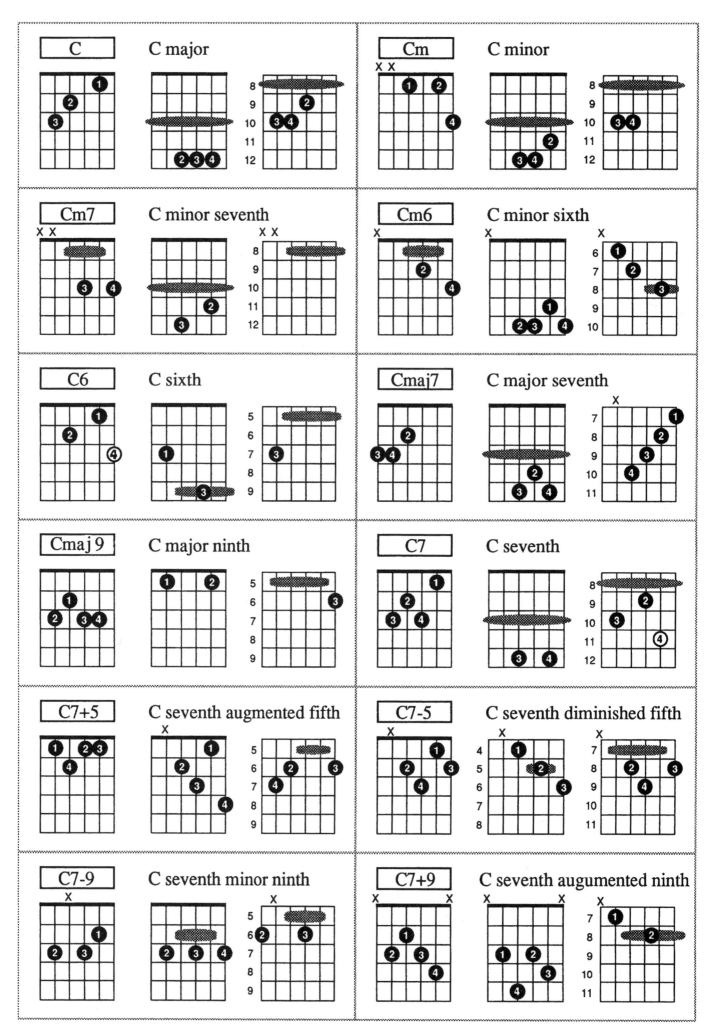

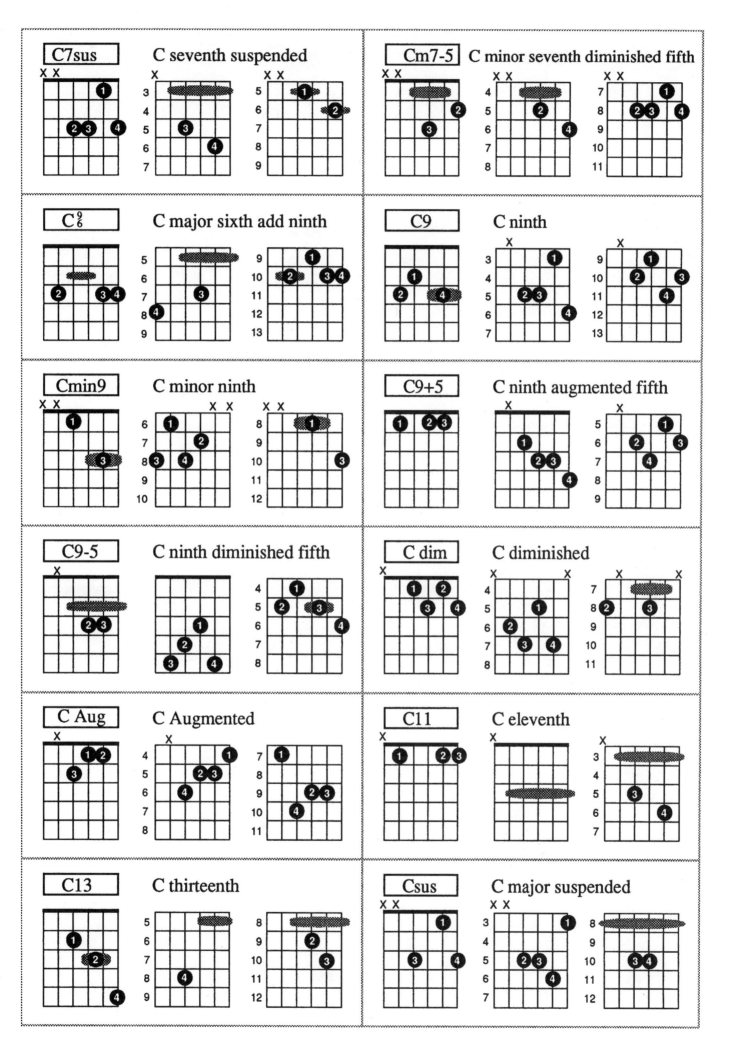

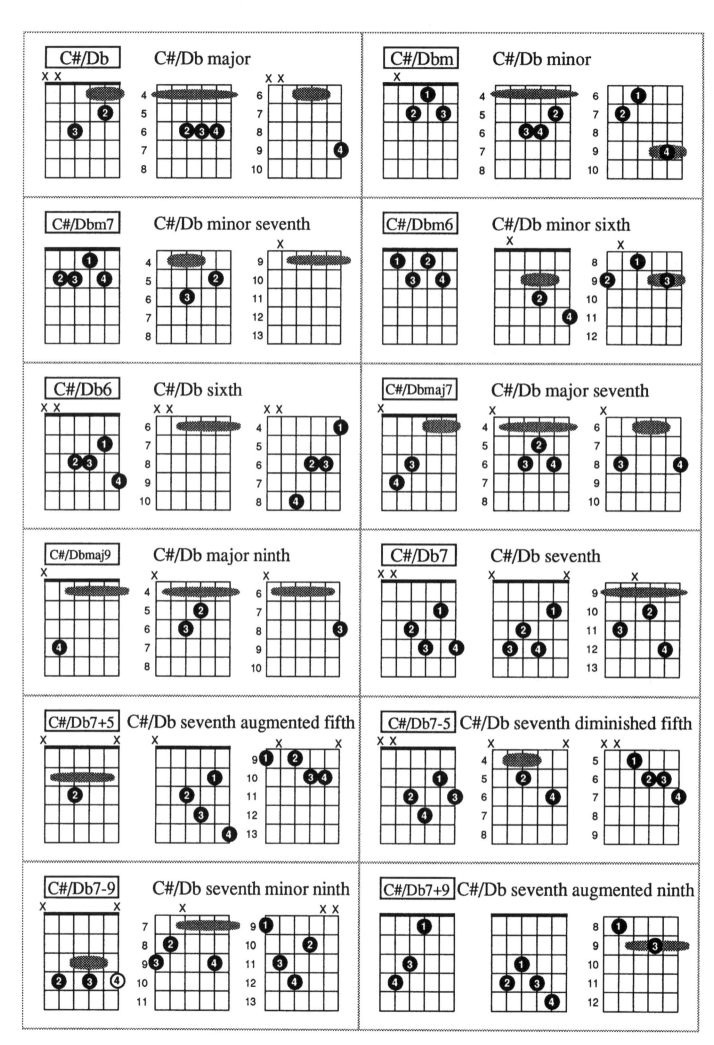

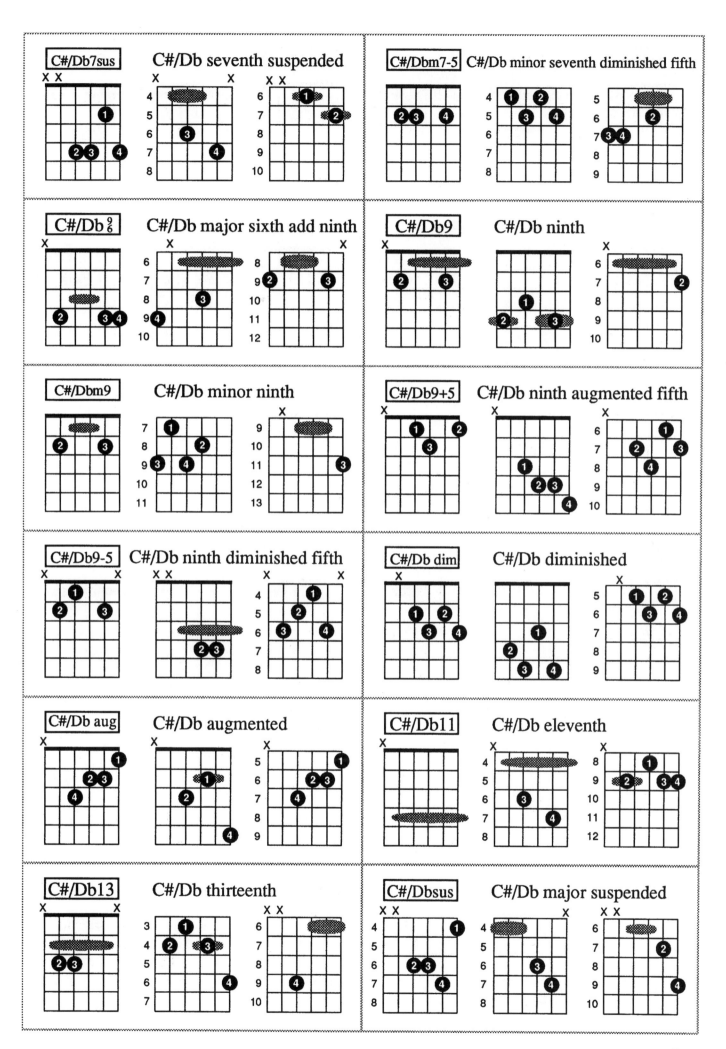

7

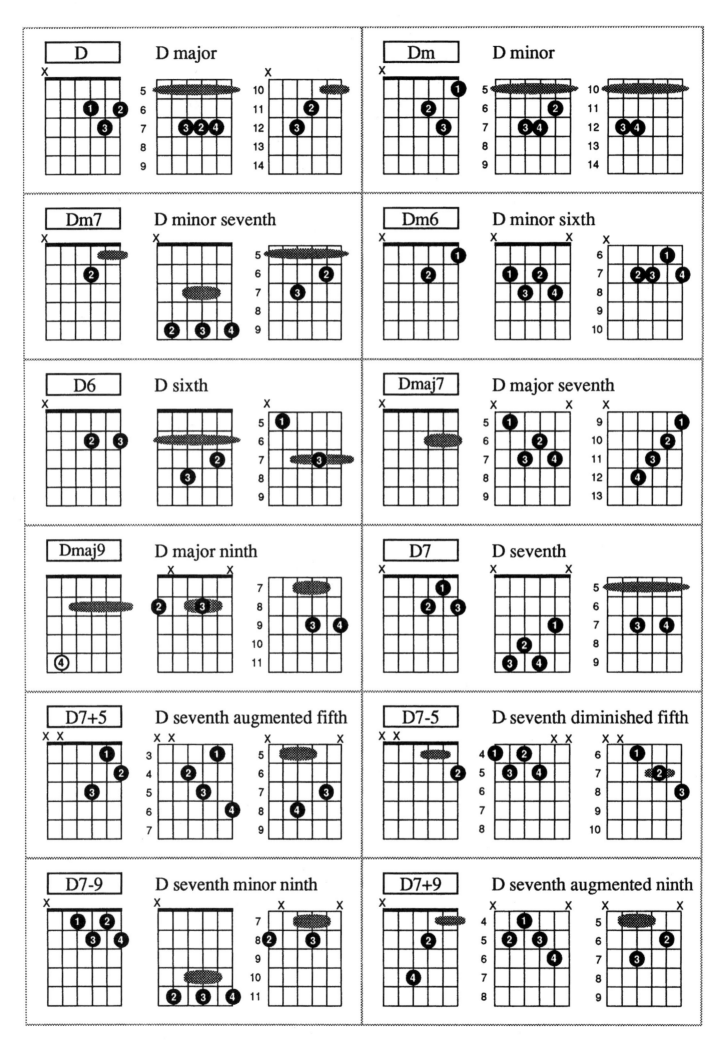

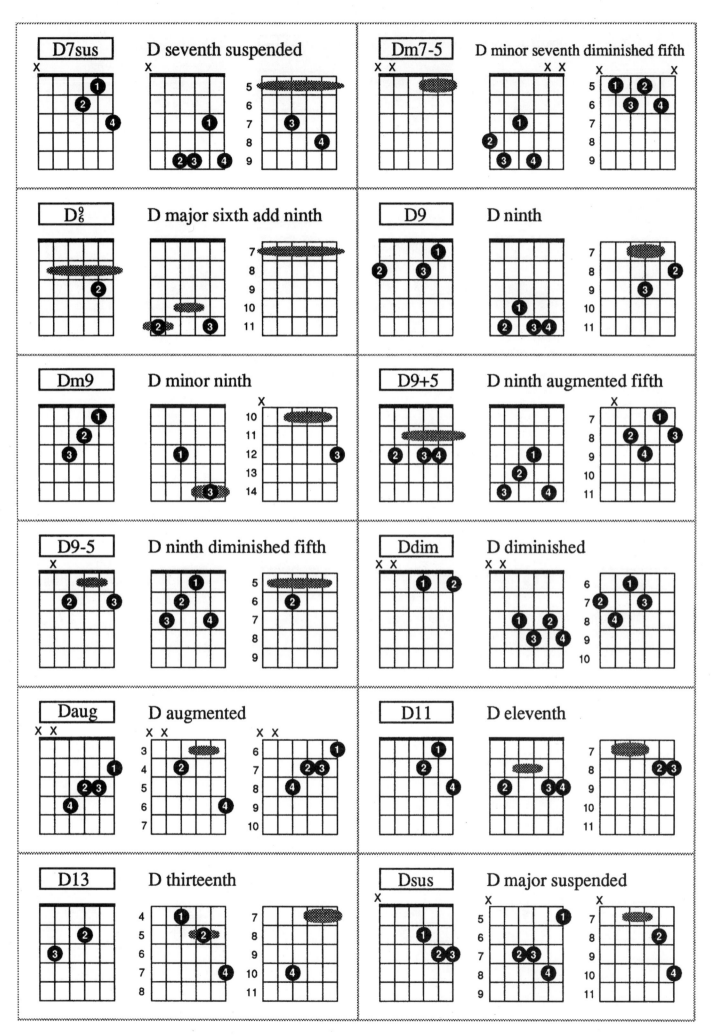

D7sus — D seventh suspended

Dm7-5 — D minor seventh diminished fifth

D⁹₆ (D 9/6) — D major sixth add ninth

D9 — D ninth

Dm9 — D minor ninth

D9+5 — D ninth augmented fifth

D9-5 — D ninth diminished fifth

Ddim — D diminished

Daug — D augmented

D11 — D eleventh

D13 — D thirteenth

Dsus — D major suspended

9

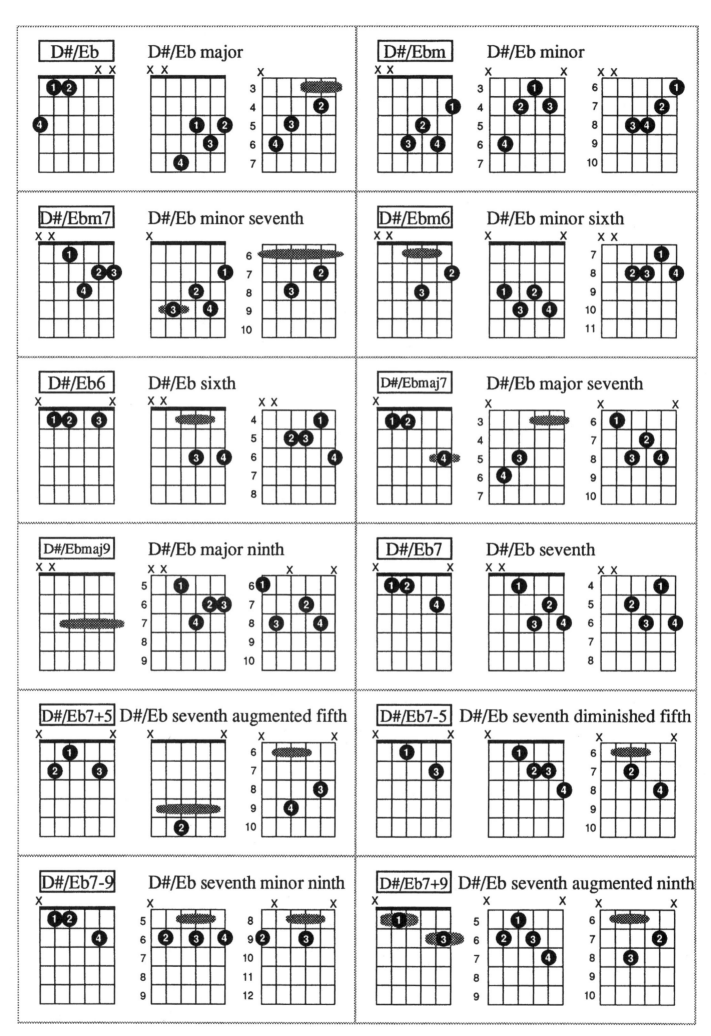

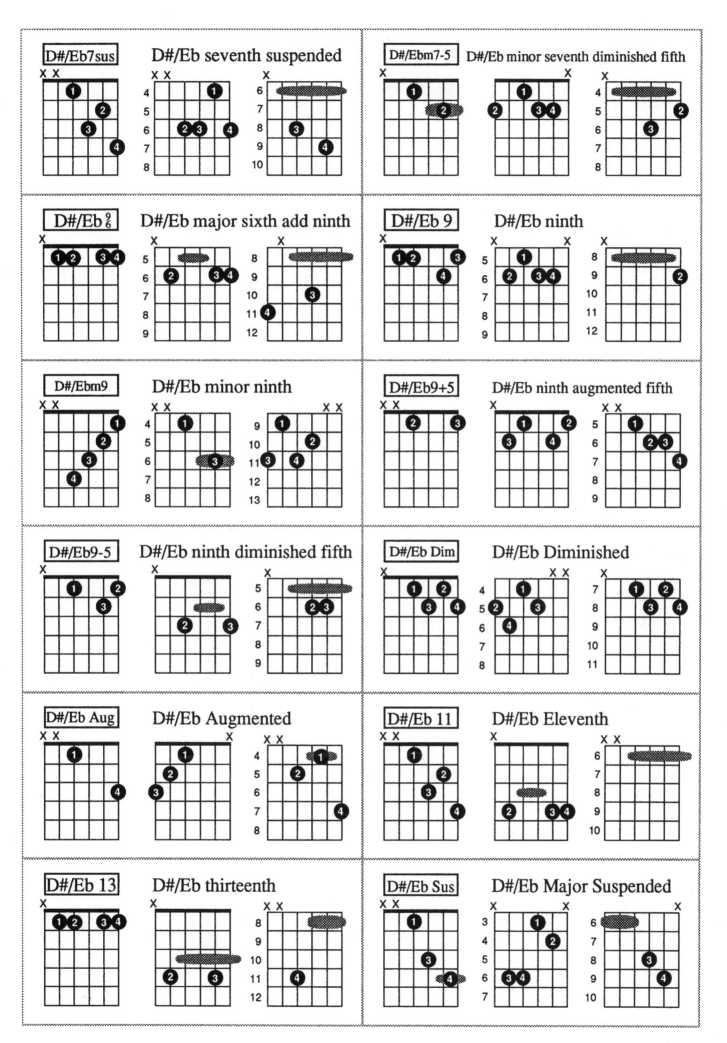

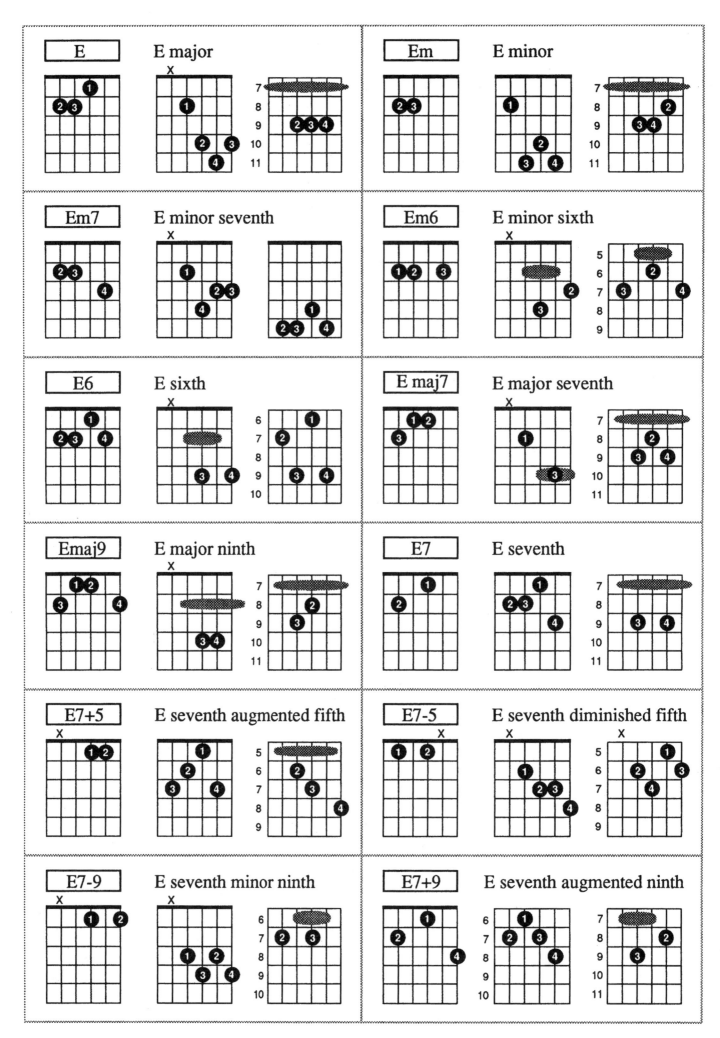

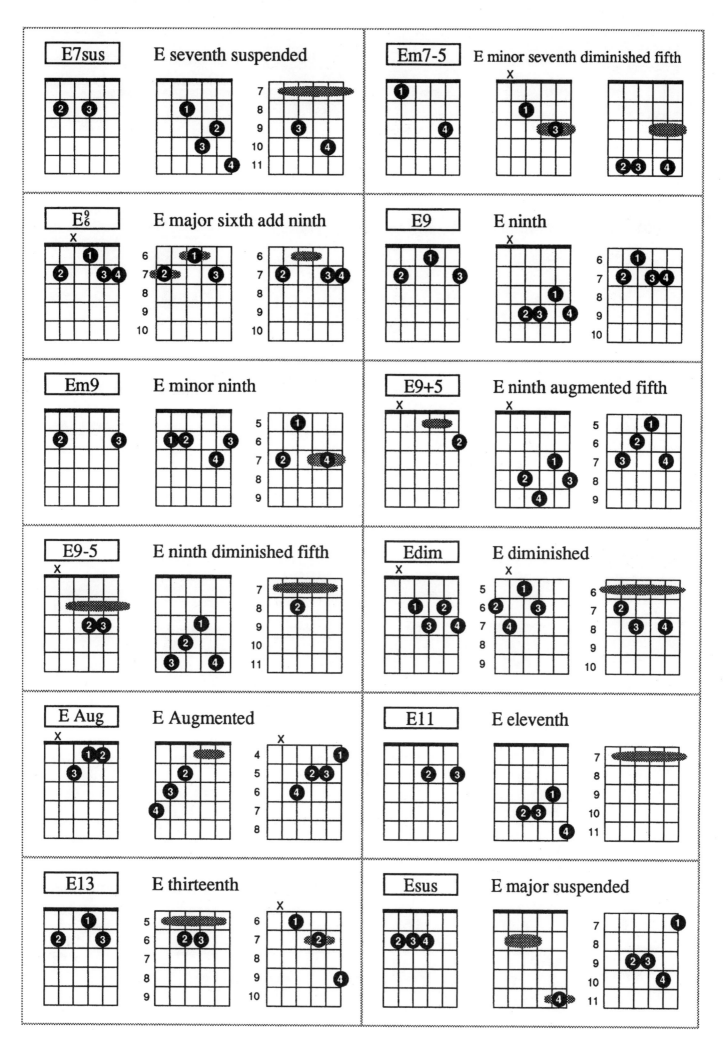

E7sus — E seventh suspended

Em7-5 — E minor seventh diminished fifth

E⁹₆ — E major sixth add ninth

E9 — E ninth

Em9 — E minor ninth

E9+5 — E ninth augmented fifth

E9-5 — E ninth diminished fifth

Edim — E diminished

E Aug — E Augmented

E11 — E eleventh

E13 — E thirteenth

Esus — E major suspended

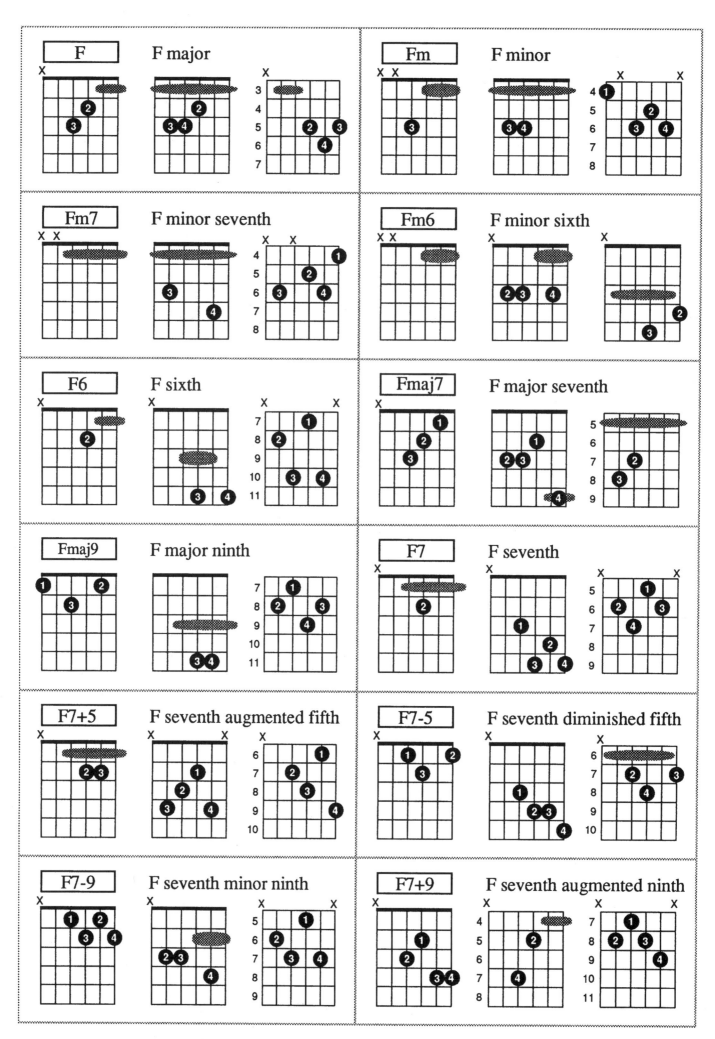

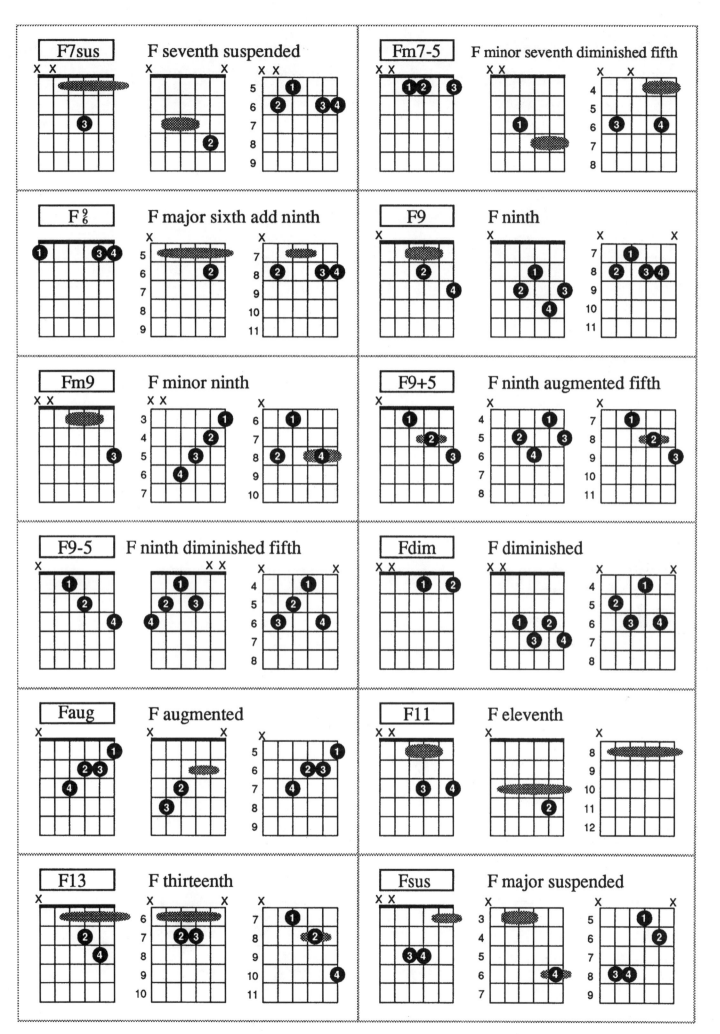

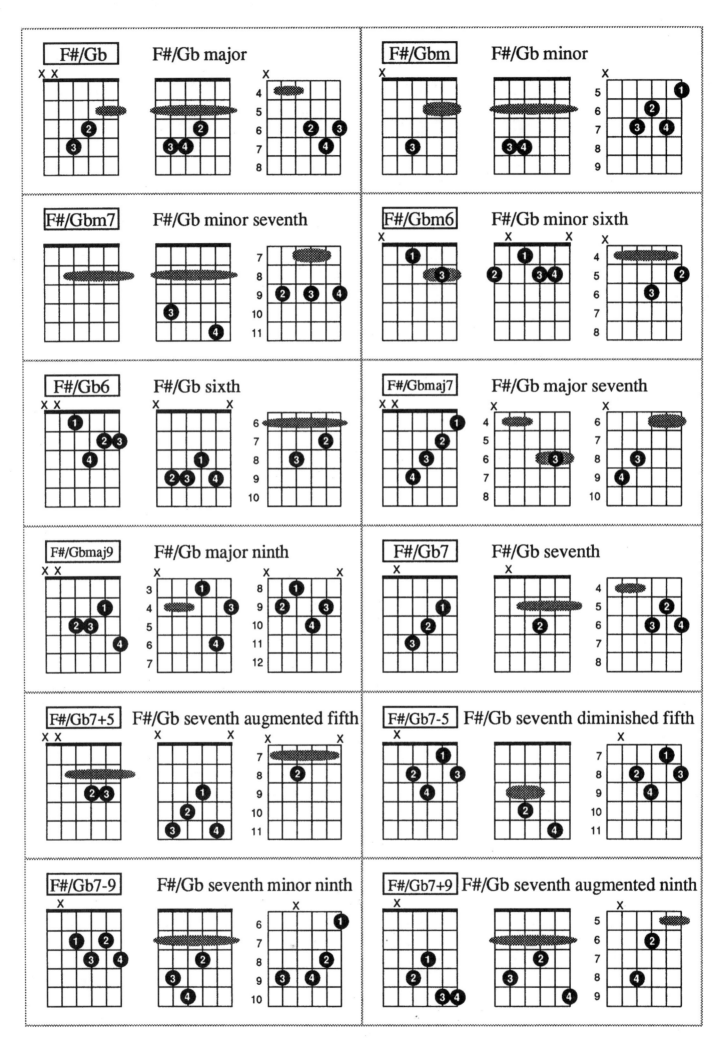

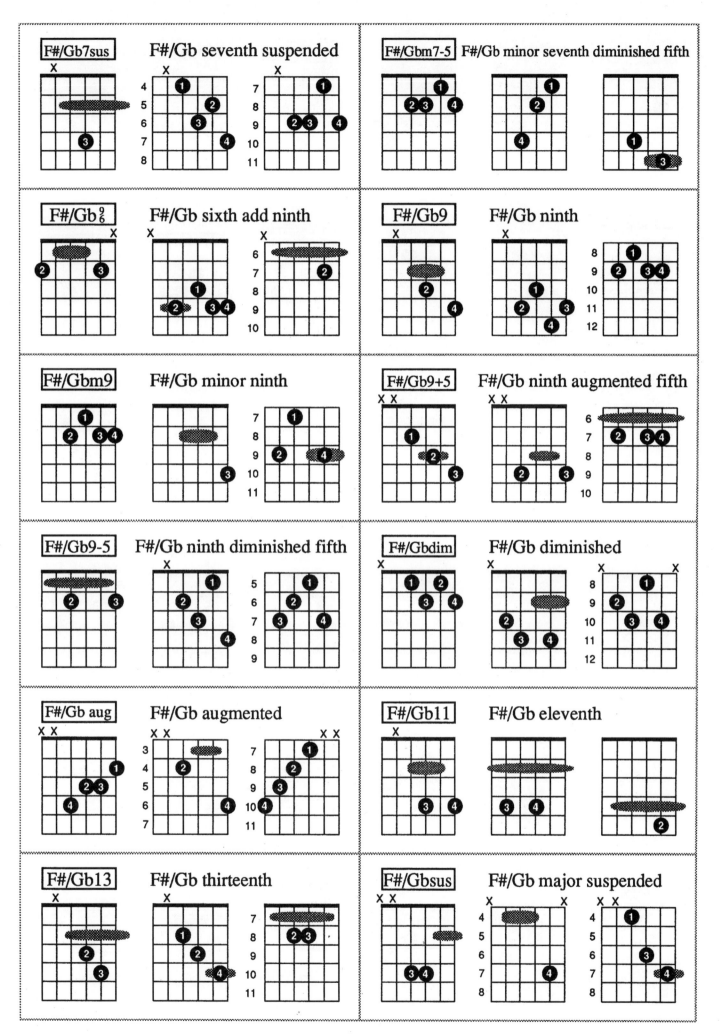

F#/Gb7sus — F#/Gb seventh suspended

F#/Gbm7-5 — F#/Gb minor seventh diminished fifth

F#/Gb 9/6 — F#/Gb sixth add ninth

F#/Gb9 — F#/Gb ninth

F#/Gbm9 — F#/Gb minor ninth

F#/Gb9+5 — F#/Gb ninth augmented fifth

F#/Gb9-5 — F#/Gb ninth diminished fifth

F#/Gbdim — F#/Gb diminished

F#/Gb aug — F#/Gb augmented

F#/Gb11 — F#/Gb eleventh

F#/Gb13 — F#/Gb thirteenth

F#/Gbsus — F#/Gb major suspended

17

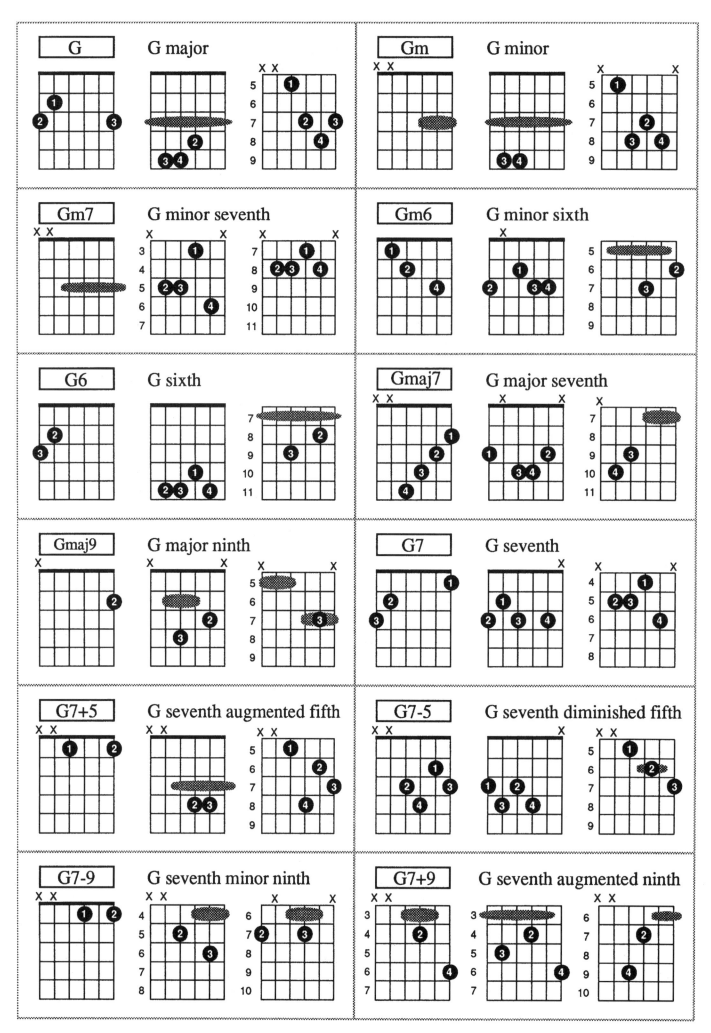

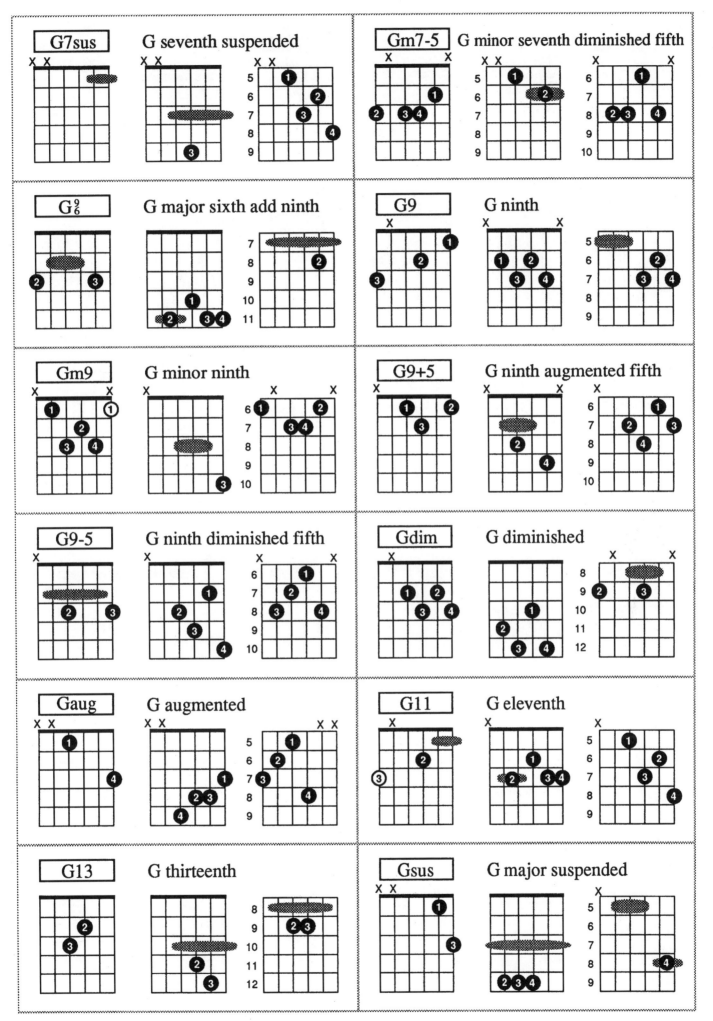

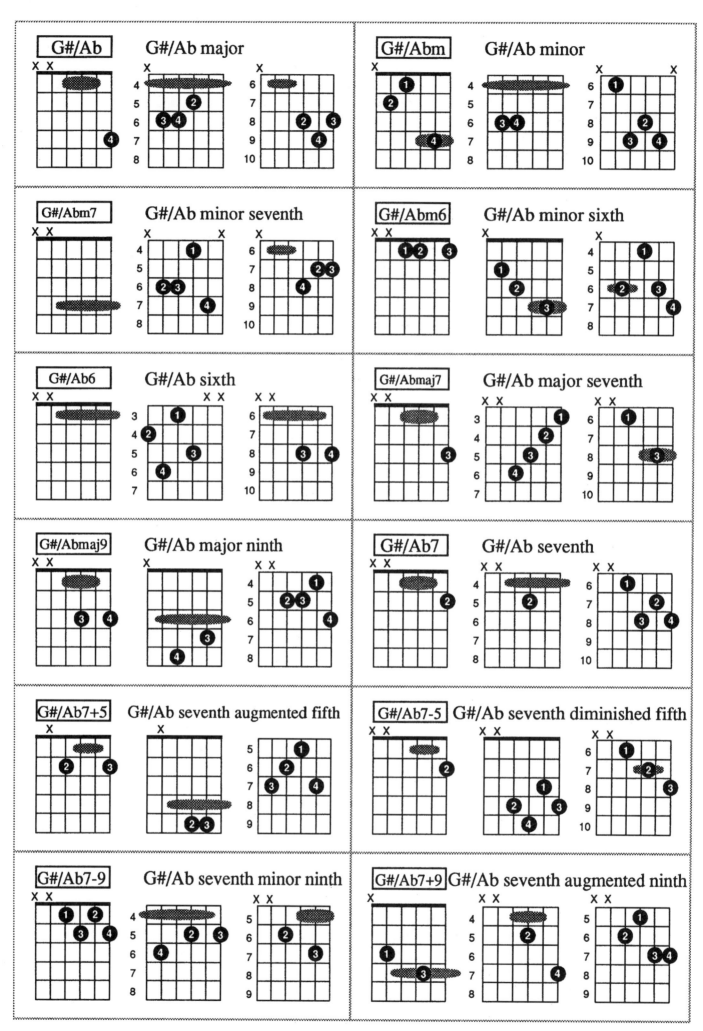

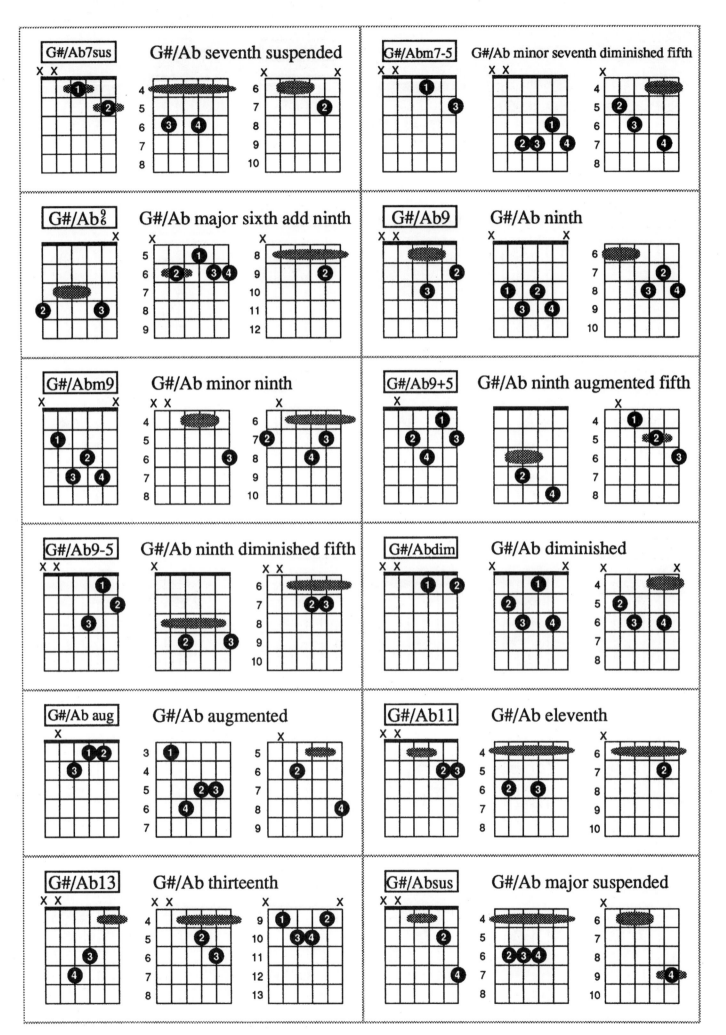

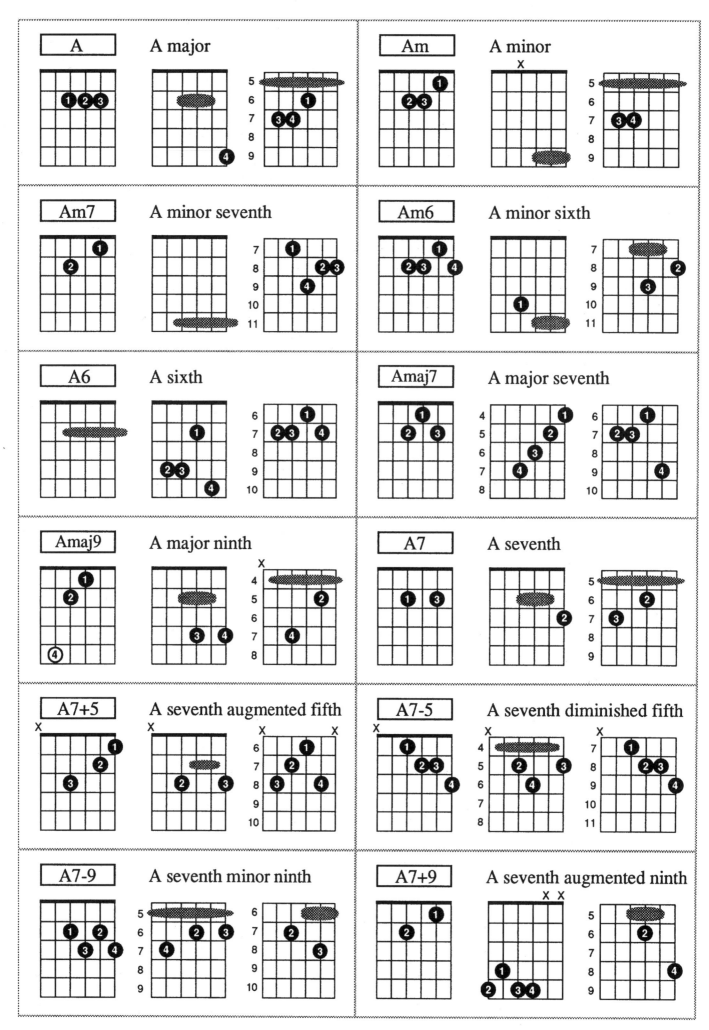

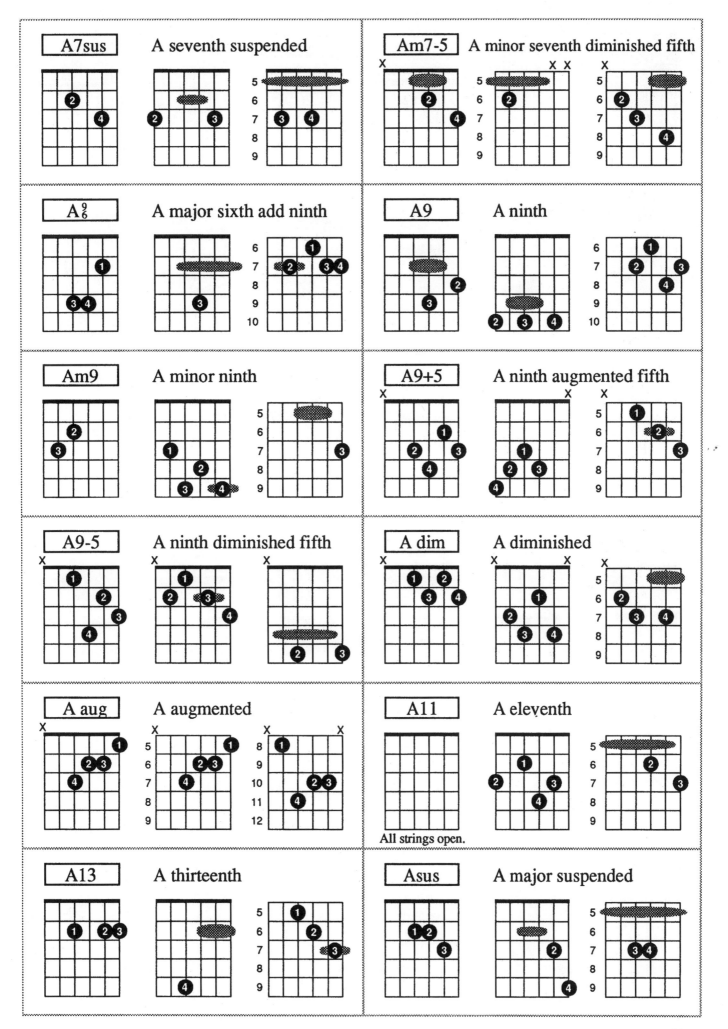

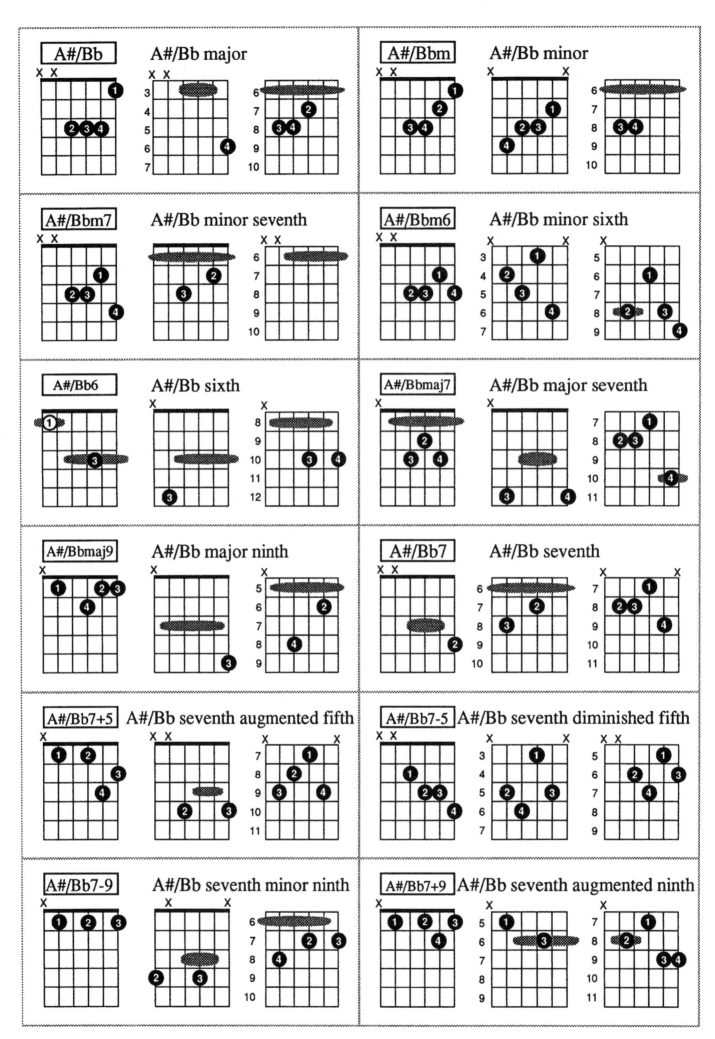

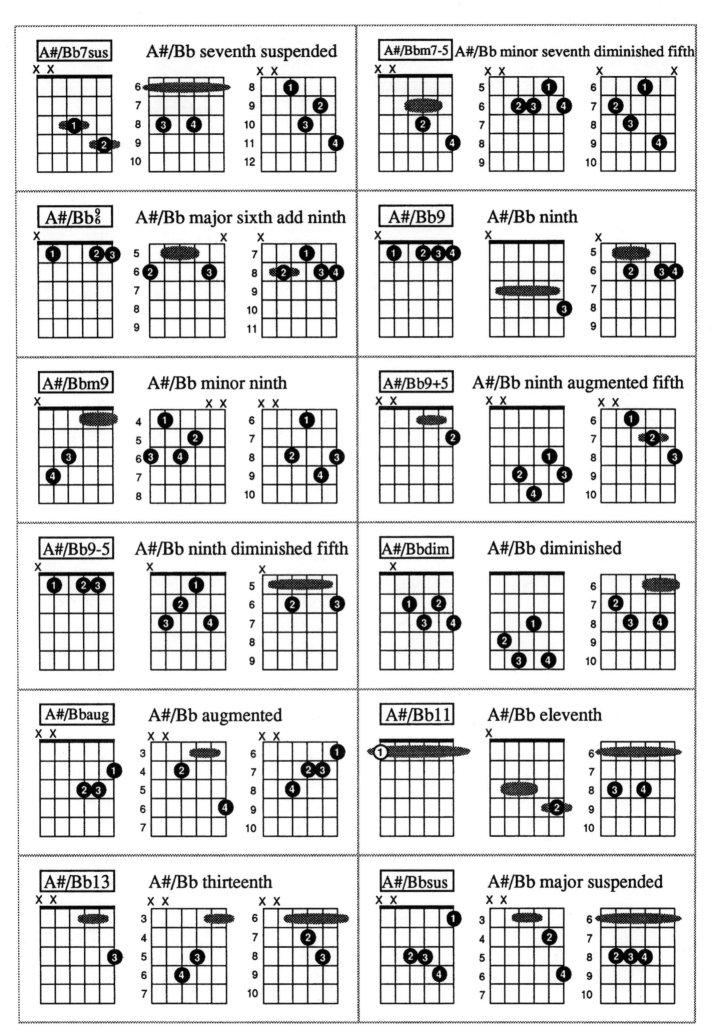

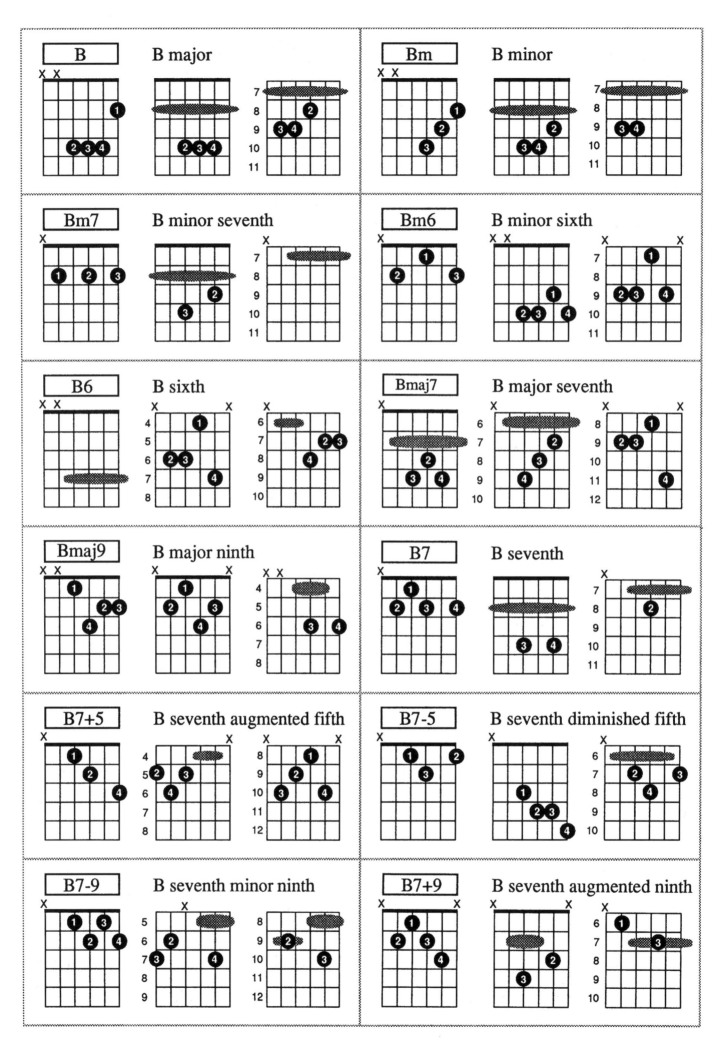

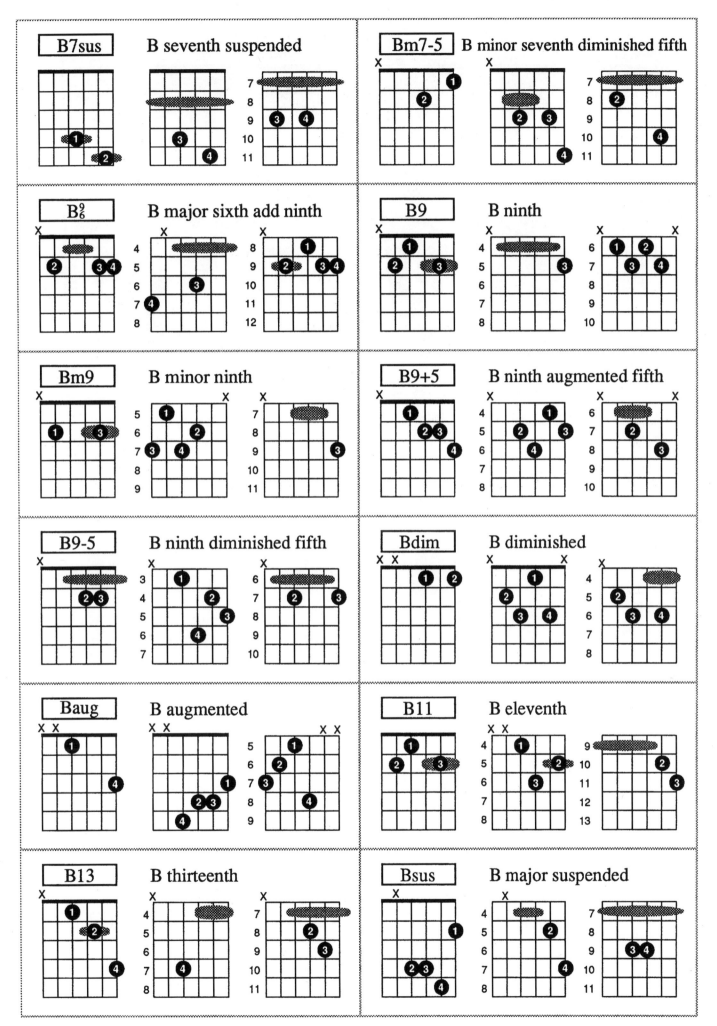

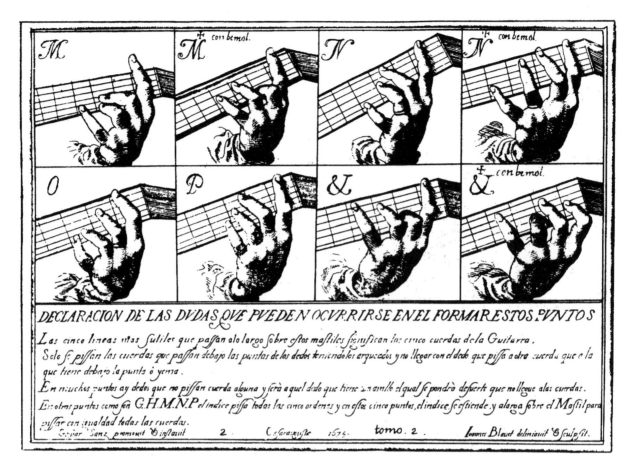

From a guitar instruction book by Gaspar Sanz, 1675.